mainstreaming children with learning disabilities

by
ferris o. henson, II
university of idaho

thomas n. fairchild
university of idaho

thomas n. fairchild
series editor

danial b. fairchild
thomas n. fairchild
illustrators

LEARNING CONCEPTS
2501 N. Lamar, Austin, Texas 78705 (512) 474-6911

Library of Congress Cataloging in Publication Data

Henson, Ferris O
　　Mainstreaming children with learning disabilities.

　　(Mainstreaming series)
　　1.　Learning disabilities.　I.　Fairchild, Thomas N.,
joint author.　II.　Title.
LC4704.H46　　　　　371.9　　　　　76-50641
ISBN 0-89384-009-2

Learning Concepts
2501 N. Lamar
Austin, Texas 78705
(512) 474-6911

Copyright© 1976 by Ferris O. Henson, II, Ph.D., Thomas N. Fairchild, Ph.D. and Danial B. Fairchild. All Rights Reserved. Printed in the United States of America. No part of this publication may be reproduced, stored in a retrieval system or transmitted, in any form or by any means, electronic, mechanical, photocopying, recording, or otherwsie, without written permission of the publisher.

To
Carolyn and Leatha

acknowledgments

As I sit at my desk looking at the manuscript which consumed so much time and energy, I would like to sincerely express my appreciation to Ferris Henson for being my friend and dropping everything to assist me; my wife, Carolyn, for her constant encouragement and support; and last *but* not least Marcy Taylor, for typing the rough, the final, and proofreading it all. She has worked as hard on the manuscript as anyone.

THOMAS N. FAIRCHILD

preface

In the past, the educational needs of exceptional children were met by removing them from the "mainstream" of the regular classrooms, and serving them in a variety of segregated self-contained special classes. The trend in the '70's is educating exceptional children in the least restrictive educational setting; that is, as close as possible to their normal peers. This concept of "mainstreaming" exceptional children has received considerable support from within and outside the educational community. Although self-contained special classes will always be a meaningful alternative for some children, the personal and educational needs of many exceptional children can better be served in the regular class program with the supportive services of ancillary personnel and/or resource room help.

With the emphasis on "mainstreaming," the regular classroom teacher is now expected to meet the needs of exceptional children in his or her classroom along with all the other children in the class. The problem is that most regular classroom teachers have little or no preparation in the area of educating exceptional children. Regular classroom teachers need basic information regarding the various exceptionalities, and more specifically, practical suggestions which they can employ to enhance the "mainstreamed" exceptional child's personal and educational development.

The MAINSTREAMING SERIES was written to fill this need. Each book in the SERIES addresses itself to one area of exceptionality allowing teachers to select from the SERIES according to their interest or need. Each text provides information designed to correct misconceptions and stereotypes, and to improve the teacher's understanding of the exceptional child's uniqueness. Numerous practical suggestions are offered which will help the teacher work more effectively with the exceptional child in the "mainstream" of the regular classroom.

Currently, there is a great deal of controversy surrounding the use of categories and labels. The books in the SERIES are organized according to categories of exceptionality because the content within each book is only relevant for a child with a specific handicapping condition. The intent is not to propagate labeling; in fact, labeling children is inconsistent with the philosophy of the SERIES. The books address themselves to behaviors, and how teachers can work with these behaviors in exceptional children. The books in the SERIES are categorized—not the children. The books are categorized in order to cue teachers to the particular content for which they might be looking.

There is much truth in the old saying, "A picture is worth a thousand words." A cartoon format was used for each book in the MAINSTREAMING SERIES as a means of sustaining interest and emphasizing important concepts. The cartoon format also allows for easy, relaxed reading. We felt that teachers, being on the firing line all day, would be more likely to read and refer to our material, than to a lengthy text filled with theory and jargon. Typically cartoons exaggerate, stereotype, and focus on weaknesses. I sincerely hope that these cartoons do not offend any children, parents, or professionals, because that is not the purpose for which they were intended. They are intended to make you think.

I hope you find this book helpful in your work with mainstreamed exceptional children, or with any other children, since they are all special.

THOMAS N. FAIRCHILD
SERIES EDITOR

introduction

The concept of learning disabilities is relatively new in special education. It has only been around since the late 50's and early 60's. In the 70's we see a rapid proliferation of programs for children identified as having specific learning disabilities.

Many persons raise the question "weren't there learning disabled children in our schools prior to the late 50's?" The answer is an unequivocal "YES." There were many children who were failing in our schools as a direct result of an inherent learning problem, or as a result of situational factors which the child could not control. As we began to learn more and more about how children learn—their uniqueness, and their styles, we began to recognize a special group of children who were having academic difficulties that were not related to mental retardation. The failing learner is not a novelty of our time. He/she has been around for all time. Fortunately, our educational technology has advanced to the point where children with learning disabilities can be identified and provided with educational experiences that will enable them to achieve academic success.

Learning disabilities are probably the most controversial area in the field of special education. There is considerable disagreement regarding the definition of learning disabilities, the causes of learning disabilities, and the remediational techniques which should be employed. Special education programs and services for learning disabled children have mushroomed as the prevalence figures have continued to rise. The current state of affairs in the area of learning disabilities is that programs for learning disabled children are serving an overwhelmingly large number of nonlearning disabled children. Because the definition is so general and vague it has been easy to "fit" many children into the definition in order to provide them with needed individual attention.

Unfortunately, this has reinforced and perpetuated the attitude that if a child is not learning at grade level using grade level materials, he or she should be receiving special educational services. Frequently when a child does not succeed in the regular classroom situation it is assumed that he or she has a "problem." It is believed that there is something "wrong" with the child and he or she is sent to a special education program. Some refer to this as the "disordered child" viewpoint. Obviously, there are children with disorders, but there are also large numbers of "nondisordered" children receiving special services. If we always assume that a child is having a learning problem becaue of an inherent disorder, we forget to look for other possible explanations for the child's learning problem, e.g., our teaching methodology, inappropriate curriculum, or other factors that are operating in the child's environment.

Mainstreaming requires that regular classroom teachers accept greater responsibility for children who are not succeeding. Many special education programs are full of children who do not belong there.

The majority of learning disabled children spend most of their time in the regular class program anyway, so what we are concerned with is providing regular classroom teachers with information and suggestions that will help them work more effectively with children who are experiencing learning difficulties. After reading this material, we hope you will have a better understanding of the learning disabled child's uniqueness, and some of the causal factors involved. We hope you will understand the issues surrounding the concept of learning disabilities, and recognize the advantages and disadvantages of the two main approaches of providing services to learning disabled children. Most importantly, we hope that the chapter on teaching children with learning problems provides you with some useful suggestions for working with this child. Remember, the suggestions can be employed even if a child does not have the categorical label "specific learning disabilities" attached to him/or her.

THOMAS N. FAIRCHILD & FERRIS O. HENSON, II

contents

1. what is the concept "learning disability?"

2. learning disabilities vs. teaching disabilities

3. controversy regarding educational programming

4. how to teach children with learning problems

chapter 1

---

what is the concept "learning disability?"

Over the years there has been much concern as to just what constitutes a "Learning Disability." Because of so much conflicting data one may question whether such a disability exists. One thing is certain, if a child is not learning, we as teachers must question the validity of our teaching strategy. We must keep changing our strategies until we get the desired performance from the child. If we do not try alternative strategies we must be concerned with a teaching disability rather than a learning disability.

Traditionally the approach to learning disabilities has been one of causal orientation. This approach has grown out of the interests of medical research. For educators, however, another approach is necessary; what can *we* do for a brain damaged child in our classroom? Educators need a model which looks at the variables of learning in order to enhance learning. The model must be flexible enough to take into account the individual differences in learning among children. Such a model is presented.

In this chapter we will discuss the present definition of learning disabilities and the characteristics that are typically associated with the term learning disabilities.

Let's take a brief look at some of the labels typically applied to children with learning problems. Some you will notice grew out of the causal approach while others grew out of an effectual approach.

PERCEPTUALLY HANDICAPPED

As this term suggests, a child may exhibit a perceptual problem that interferes with his/her learning. This might be in the auditory or visual perception area, or manifested in a perceptual-motor problem. This term was not comprehensive enough because all children with learning disabilities do not have perceptual problems.

ORGANIC BRAIN DAMAGE

This cause oriented approach implies that a child's brain is actually damaged. Interestingly enough, very few children labeled as "learning disabled" show any neurological signs of brain damage when medically examined!

MINIMAL BRAIN DAMAGE

Since most children labeled as "learning disabled" show no neurological signs of brain damage, the term minimal damage was incorporated. This implies that the damage must be there, but it is minimal and therefore cannot be detected by modern neurology!

MINIMAL CEREBRAL DYSFUNCTION

The term minimal brain damage was later discarded for the term minimal cerebral dysfunction primarily to move away from the concept of brain damage, but to still emphasize neurological dysfunctioning.

DYSLEXIA/READING DISABILITY

These terms grew out of an effectual approach. While these terms offer no data to aid in remediation, it does imply the problem is in reading rather than the brain.

DYSCALCULIA

As another effectual oriented term, dyscalculia offers no clues as to remediation. But the problem here is in arithmetic, not the central nervous system.

As you can see, the labels go on and on. However, these labels do not aid you in the classroom. The terms that will help you the most with any child are terms which describe the child's performance on a variety of tasks. (This will be dealt with in Chapter 4.) Now, however, let's look a little deeper into the concept "Learning Disabilities."

"Children with specific learning disabilities exhibit a disorder in one or more of the basic psychological processes involved in understanding or in using spoken or written language. These may be manifested in disorders of listening, thinking, talking, reading, writing, spelling, or arithmetic. They include conditions which have been referred to as perceptual handicaps, brain injury, minimal brain dysfunction, dyslexia, developmental aphasia, etc. They do not include learning problems which are due primarily to visual, hearing, or motor handicaps, to mental retardation, emotional disturbance or to environmental deprivation."

Adopted by Congress as part of the "Children with Specific Learning Disabilities Act of 1969."

What is the Concept of Learning Disability?

Since we are dealing with children in the regular classroom, we need not worry about definitions which enable us to classify children. There is, however, one characteristic which, according to many experts, stands out among the rest. That characteristic is "discrepancy."

Discrepancy refers to a gap between how one expects a given child to perform and how that child is actually performing. A more common term is *underachieving.*

Of course, these expectations must be in line with what is reasonable. We need evidence that the child is capable of achieving at a higher level. Usually this is determined by some set of norms.

Some experts state that an educationally significant discrepancy is one in which a primary grade child is behind one to one and one-half years in reading, math, spelling, or writing. For older children a two-year gap is considered significant.

But, ultimately what good is it to even show these discrepancies? If a child is two years behind, or three months behind, we still only have one job; and that job is to teach the child. When a child is not succeeding it is too tempting to put the blame on the child. All children can learn, and our responsibility is to find out how to promote learning in each individual child.

If we take this approach, our assessment techniques must be problem-solving oriented. The only good assessment is one that shows us how to try various solutions to get a child to learn. What good is it to know if a child is two years behind in a given subject area unless we have specific prescriptions for teaching? What good does it do to label the child? The labels *do not* tell us how to alter our teaching strategies.

Characteristics

While our main concern as a teacher is to produce learning in our children, there are certain behaviors that children display that interfere with the learning process. We must detect these behaviors and change them so they will cease to have a detrimental effect on learning. Typically these behaviors occur in the following areas:

- Activity level of behavior
- On-task behavior
- Motor behavior
- Visual perception
- Auditory perception
- Language problems
- Social behavior
- Orientation behavior
- Academic behavior

DON'T READ THE FINE PRINT!

All children display some of the behaviors listed above. If a child displays some of these behaviors, do not label him/her "Learning Disabled." Rather work to increase or decrease these behaviors!

Activity Level

The activity level can take either of the two extremes. The hyperactive child is overly active...

...while the hypoactive child responds very slowly.

On-Task Behavior

Some children have not been reinforced in the past for paying attention to a task. Many times assignments given are too long for the child's attention level, thus producing failure. Sometimes a child will repeat a simple task over and over again. The child may often be easily distracted.

Motor Behavior

Problems related to motor behavior are poor coordination in both fine and gross motor activity; poor tactile discrimination; and kinesthetic problems related to inaccuracy in reaching for, and grasping objects. Writing problems also fall into this category.

Visual Perception

A child with problems in visual perception may not be able to discriminate visual stimuli accurately (substitutes "b" for "d" or cannot discriminate between an object and its background), and may not be able to recall previously presented visual stimuli.

Auditory Perception

In the area of auditory perception the child may not be able to discriminate between the background noise and the main sound source. This child may also have problems understanding spoken language as it may be difficult to discriminate between letters, words, and sentences. Auditory recall may also be poor.

Language Problems

A child may have difficulty in expressing ideas. Sometimes he/she may be unable to put words in the correct sequential order, or may have problems with grammar.

REMEMBER

Children from some para-cultures may use dialects different from the Anglo-American dialect.

Social

Social behavior problems may take the form of inappropriately touching other people, acting impulsively without considering the consequence of the behavior, or throwing temper tantrums.

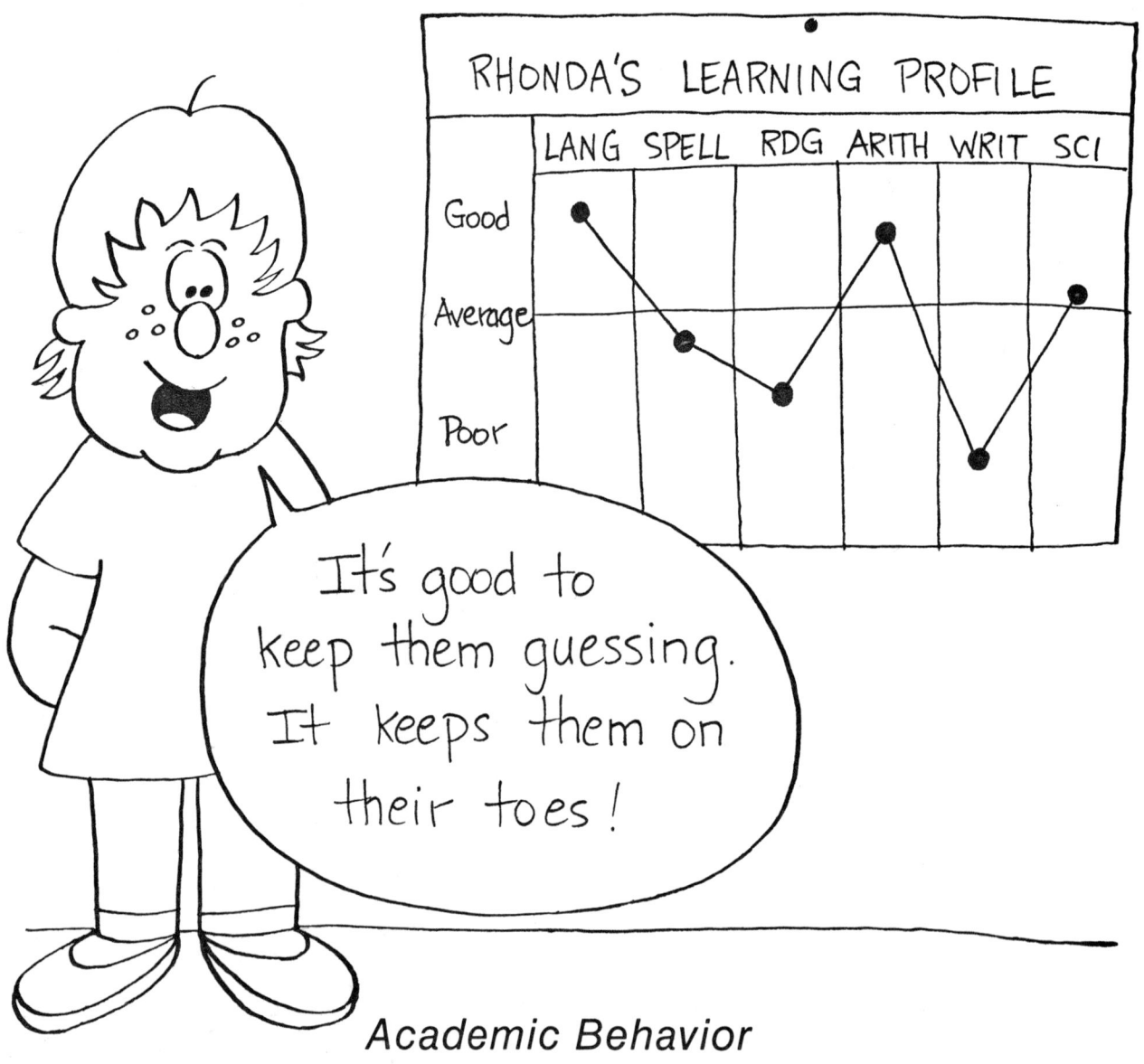

Academic Behavior

A child may be extremely poor in some academic areas, while average or good in others. Some discrepancies across academic areas occur in most children, but if an extreme discrepancy is observed an immediate evaluation of the child's performance, the teaching strategies, and reinforcement used, is in order. For some reason, different strategies may have to be used in the extremely poor areas. A more frequent schedule of reinforcement may also have to be used.

Orientation Behavior

This behavior deals with poor discrimination between left and right,...

...judging distance, or judging size. Problems with temporal concepts may also occur. These would involve problems in sequencing past, present, and future events.

While there are still some researchers concerned with the causes of learning disabilities, data thus far does not indicate any relevant educational findings. The approach having the most applicable data is the one which looks at a given child's behavior and then systematically applies solutions and measures change.

chapter 2

---

learning disabilities vs. teaching disabilities

Anytime parents and educators are discussing learning disabilities, there is always a need to know "why?" "Why my child?" "What causes learning disabilities anyway?"

The causes of children's learning problems can be separated into three major categories:

> Intrapersonal factors
> ("True" learning disabilities)
>
> Personal factors
> (Child "owns" part of the problem)
>
> Extrapersonal factors
> (Instructional or teaching disabilities)

Intrapersonal Factors

There are children who exhibit learning problems as a result of some inherent problem within the child. These are the children with "true" learning disabilities.

These learning disabilities are the result of some neurological dysfunctioning, which can be attributed to any or several of the following: (1) biochemical irregularities; (2) subtle perinatal brain damage; (3) circulatory, toxic, or metabolic functioning difficulties as a result of disease during prenatal development; (4) illnesses or injuries sustained during development and maturation of the central nervous system; (5) developmental or maturational lags; and (6) inherited familial traits.

Personal Factors

Personal factors responsible for contributing to learning problems are included to emphasize that some children need to accept responsibility for the problems they are experiencing.

A child who does not have an inherent problem, and is receiving "super" teaching, may be doing poorly because of unidentified needs, interests, attitudes, and motivations.

Some children who are capable of learning, and who receive good instruction and teaching tend to fall farther and farther behind because they aren't interested or they don't care. It doesn't take too long before the gap widens and serious academic difficulties result.

Extrapersonal Factors

Extrapersonal means that although the child is experiencing learning difficulties, they are primarily the result of factors outside of the child and beyond his/her control. Some special educators use the terms "instructional disabilities," and "teaching disabilities" to emphasize that the problem is not inherent in the child, but instead is environmentally or situationally based. These children are not "truly" learning disabled, but they still have learning problems.

Extrapersonal factors include such things as inappropriate teaching methodology, inappropriate materials and curriculum, and lack of individualization.

There *are* children who have learning disabilities which are a result of intrapersonal factors, such as the types that were mentioned earlier. Personal factors which were mentioned result in learning problems for other children. However, these children are a minority of the children that have been diagnosed as learning disabled. The majority are children who are having learning problems which are related to extrapersonal factors.

Estimates regarding how many of our school-aged children have specific learning disabilities range from 1% to as high as 40%. Obviously, different educators are emphasizing different causal factors when incidence figures are this discrepant. The lower incidence figures might realistically reflect the prevalence of children with inherent learning problems, but by no stretch of the imagination is it possible to say that 40% of our school-aged children have some inherent learning problem that is causing them trouble with academics.

Although there are intrapersonal causes of learning disabilities in children, they are a minority.

Learning disabilities has become a wastebasket definition. Because it is so general and vague you can make a lot of children fit the definition.

Because the label and the services for learning disabled children have been and continue to be abused, large numbers of nonlearning disabled children are inappropriately diagnosed and provided service in L. D. programs.

Some children who are not learning disabled are purposefully labeled "L. D." in order to provide them with the individual help or tutoring that they might need.

We're not saying that it's wrong to give children individual attention, but the intention of the resource room is to work with "truly" exceptional children, not with any child having academic difficulties. They are the responsibility of regular education.

In some cases attaching the label "learning disability" becomes an easy out for teachers. If a child is not learning up to par, there must be something wrong with the child, so he is "farmed out." Teachers neglect taking a look at personal and extrapersonal factors which may be causing or contributing to the problem.

Because of our tendency to attach the "learning disability" label onto any child who is having academic problems, programs and services for these children have mushroomed.

Children are placed on waiting lists to receive help from the resource room. In the meantime everyone ignores the problem waiting for the resource room mystical cure.

The most serious problem related to our eagerness to label is that learning disabilities programs are now overcrowded and have waiting lists. Large numbers of children in these programs and on the waiting lists are nonlearning disabled. As a consequence, many "true" learning disabled children who desperately need services are not receiving help.

Recognizing that L. D. educational programs are serving a large number of nonlearning disabled children, the Federal Government is putting a limit on the number of children that are eligible for state funds under the classification learning disability. This is an effort to assure that "true" learning disabled children receive the services that are available.

Remember, regardless of the causes of the child's learning problems, you are responsible for the child's education. Even if the child requires and receives special services, chances are high that he/she will spend time in your regular classroom. That time should be spent productively. The resource teacher can't do it all.

chapter 3

controversy regarding educational programming

The term "controversy" probably best describes the status of learning disabilities in the field of special education.

There is controversy regarding the definition, identification and classification of learning disabled children. There is also controversy regarding the causes of learning disabilities, and the types of educational programming necessary to help this child succeed academically.

Within the area of learning disabilities there are two major camps: the perceptual-motor/psycholinguistic process camp (hereafter referred to as the process camp)...

...and the behavioral/academic skills camp (hereafter referred to as the skills camp).

These camps deserve discussion because their philosophies differ regarding learning disabilities. The types of services learning disabled children receive are considerably different depending on the camp you adhere to.

Let's take a look at the general philosophies and approaches of the two camps.

The Process Camp

In the early days of learning disabilities, (late 1950's and the 1960's), the process approach was the accepted and respected way of working with learning disabled children.

The process approach reflected the influence of the medical model in special education. Traditionally, special education has been tied to the medical model. The medical model in special education has emphasized the diagnose - classify - treat/place framework. Children who were having difficulties in school were tested in order to determine *what was the matter with them* that was interfering with their academic success. They were then classified (labeled) and placed in a special classroom consonant with their label. The most popular form of treatment at the time was taking children out of the regular program and putting them in self-contained special classes.

Thus, children classified as having learning disabilities, were perceived as having *inherent* problems e.g., minimal cerebral dysfunction, which were interfering with their successful performance. There was something wrong with the child, either in the perceptual-motor area, or in the processing of language.

Since the learning disabilities were attributed to an inherent problem in the child and they were a direct result of perceptual-motor or processing problems, the primary mode of treatment in the 60's was remediation of these perceptual-motor and processing problems. Once perceptual-motor or processing problems were remediated, learning could then take place.

So, in the 60's children identified as learning disabled spent many hours in self-contained classes and resource room programs in an effort to remediate perceptual-motor deficiencies. Activities and programs suggested by Frostig, Kephart, Barsch, and Doman-Delecato were popular. The assumption underlying these approaches was that perceptual-motor skills would improve and as a consequence reading could then improve.

The research to date has not been supportive in showing that tracing, walking down balance beams, doing snow-angels, and crawling contributes to a child's development of reading skills.

The process camp also attributes learning disabilities to a breakdown in the processing of language. The child may not be receiving information accurately through the visual or auditory pathways; may not be integrating or associating the information correctly; or may not be able to express himself well verbally or manually. The psycholinguistic process approach is centered primarily around the I.T.PA. (Illinois Test of Psycholinguistic Abilities) because it is the most comprehensive assessment instrument for identifying specific processing difficulties. Once these difficulties are isolated, they are assumed to be the causes of the child's learning problems. The process difficulties are then remediated, using the mountains of material available in I.T.P.A. remediation guidelines, or texts on psycholinguistic training. Persons in the process camp assume that successful learning can take place only after processing problems have been remediated.

Again, the research has not been highly supportive of the effectiveness of remediating psycholinguistic processes in an attempt to improve academic skills.

The Skills Camp

The skills camp emerged in the early 1970's, and has become a powerful influence on current practices in learning disabilities.

The skills camp emerged as a result of the dissatisfaction with the process camp's approach and it's ineffectiveness in meeting the needs of children identified as learning disabled.

The process camp seemed to be overly concerned with causes, and always perceived the problem as inherent in the child and usually a result of some type of minimal damage or cerebral dysfunction.

Persons in the skills camp do not deny the existence of children whose learning problems are the result of inherent factors, but they advocate that teachers be cognizant of situational and extrapersonal factors that are causing or contributing to the problem.

The skills camp minimizes the importance of causes and labeling anyway. In order to provide an appropriate education for a child with learning problems we must work with observable behaviors—so labeling loses it's significance and utility.

The skills camp is rapidly becoming the most popular of the two camps because of the de-emphasis on labeling, and because it focuses on observable behaviors. It remediates by focusing on the actual skills that a child does or does not possess, rather than focusing on a perceived or real internal processing problem.

An example might help to clarify the distinction between the two camps. Jimmy is a 2nd grade boy referred because he is having difficulty with reading. A member of the process camp would administer the I.T.P.A., and probably a perceptual-motor test among others. The test results may show that the child is behind his peers in perceptual-motor development, and is weak in the visual perception area. Jimmy spends time daily with a resource teacher or an aide working on perceptual-motor activities, and remedial I.T.P.A. activities. The assumption is that when Jimmy's perceptual-motor skills and visual perception skills improve, reading will improve because difficulties in these areas were interfering with Jimmy's learning to read.

A member of the skills camp would be concerned about what specific reading skills Jimmy does or does not possess. An assessment would include a diagnostic reading test and informal reading tests. The tests would help to identify what skills Jimmy possesses and what skills are deficient. If his problem is difficulty in the short vowel sounds, or applying the "CVC", "CVVC", "CVCE", rules, or comprehension, etc., then these skills are taught directly. Obviously, we have oversimplified because we have neglected teaching methods, reading materials, or approach used, etc.

The explanation of the two camps has not been very detailed. The intent was to give you some feeling for what is currently happening in the area of learning disabilities. Be aware that there are a lot of tents spread out between the two camps.

Our primary concern in the preparation of this material is how regular classroom teachers can help a child with a learning disability when he or she is in the regular classroom for most of the day. The authors will be emphasizing the skills camp because they feel educational planning from that point of view will be more successful for the regular classroom teacher and more productive for the child.

chapter 4

---

how to teach children with learning problems

A "problem-solving" approach which is generalizable across different social or academic behaviors is necessary when teaching children with diverse learning characteristics, as in the mainstreamed classroom.

The problem-solving approach involves setting specific objectives for the child, collecting a rate or duration measure on the occurrence of the child's behavior, planning and implementing a teaching or change strategy, and finally evaluating the success of the intervention.

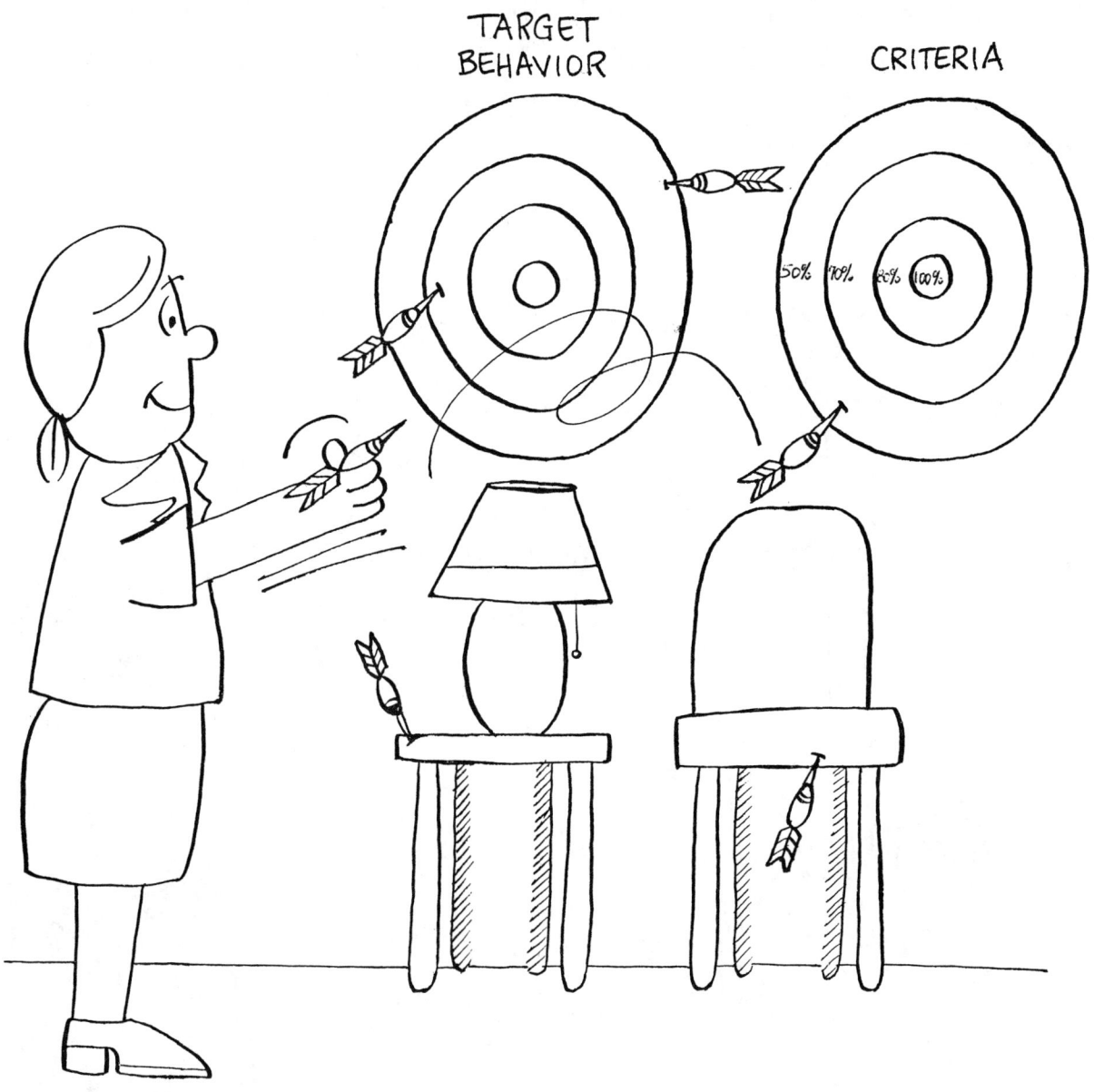

Setting specific objectives includes two steps. These are: 1) pinpointing the target behavior, and 2) setting a criteria of how frequent or infrequent we want that behavior to occur. In academic areas our criteria will also deal with the accuracy of the child's responses (e.g., discriminating between "b" and "d").

In pinpointing the problem area we can only use behaviors that are observable, otherwise how could we evaluate the program? Much concern in the area of learning disabilities has been with unmeasurable assumed concepts.

We can't observe if a child's visual perception per se improves, but we can measure if in fact, he is substituting "d" for "b" at a decreasing rate.

Due to our own habits, it may be difficult to describe what we are looking for in specific observable behaviors. We are used to describing children with terms like "aggressive," "angry," "having emotional problems," etc. These are too vague to help us plan a teaching or management strategy.

Instead of describing Rhonda as "aggressive," describe what Rhonda actually does. For example, Rhonda may strike the child sitting next to her when that child turns around and stares at her.

Describing what a child does in observable behaviors will force us also to look at events occurring before or after the specified behavior. This will give us clues as to how to deal with the specific behavior. Using Rhonda as our example again, we would want to observe if any other behaviors exhibited by other children seated near Rhonda would "cause" Rhonda to strike them. If this were the case, we could change the seating arrangement. We may find our intervention is as simple as that!

The second step in setting objectives is to judge an acceptable criterion of performance. This can be stated as a certain frequency at which we accept the behavior or a certain percent of correct or accurate responses.

Some tasks require higher accuracy than others. Older children in the 3rd grade, for example, may be required to reach an accuracy rate of 100% in naming the letters of the alphabet in manuscript style when presented visually. We may require this only 70% of the time with a kindergarten or 1st grade child. As another example, some teachers may tolerate a higher general "out of seat" classroom and set a criterion level of 5 times in 5 minutes for an overly active child. As that child gets older, or changes teachers, a lower criterion rate may be required as a "mastery" rate.

The purpose in setting objectives stated in observable behaviors is that they allow us to measure changes which are too small to measure by standardized achievement tests or other traditional norm-referenced measures.

Typically, standardized measures are used only once or twice per year to measure how much a student learns in that school year. The assumption is that a teacher teaches and the children learn at a "qualitatively" different rate. Hence, some children receive "A's" and others "F's."

An approach which sets objectives with a criteria of mastery takes a different position from the traditional approach. The assumption is that all children can learn to levels never before expected (our low expectations were in fact contributing to the children's low performance). The qualitative aspects are than controlled by the teacher. That is, for example, that all children in the class will be able to name all the letters of the alphabet when presented visually, with 100% accuracy. So, all the children are expected to do "A" quality work, the variable being the amount of time it takes a given child to reach the "mastery" level. In other words, for whatever reason, some children will reach the criteria in less time than other children.

The fact that the child's performance is described in terms of observable behaviors coupled with a daily measuring system allows for feedback to the teacher so that changes in strategy can occur within a relatively short period of time (possibly 2 weeks as compared to 9 months using the standardized test approach).

The daily measuring system consists of observing a child's behavior during the same time period of each day. This observation can be made by the teacher or, if the teacher is lucky enough, the classroom aide. The recording can take place as the behavior is occurring or at a later time if the child was writing or calculating a paper (a permanent product). The length of time involved in the "on the spot" method is usually from between 5 - 30 minutes depending on the complexity of the learning problem and the amount of time the teacher or classroom aide has to attend to the problem.

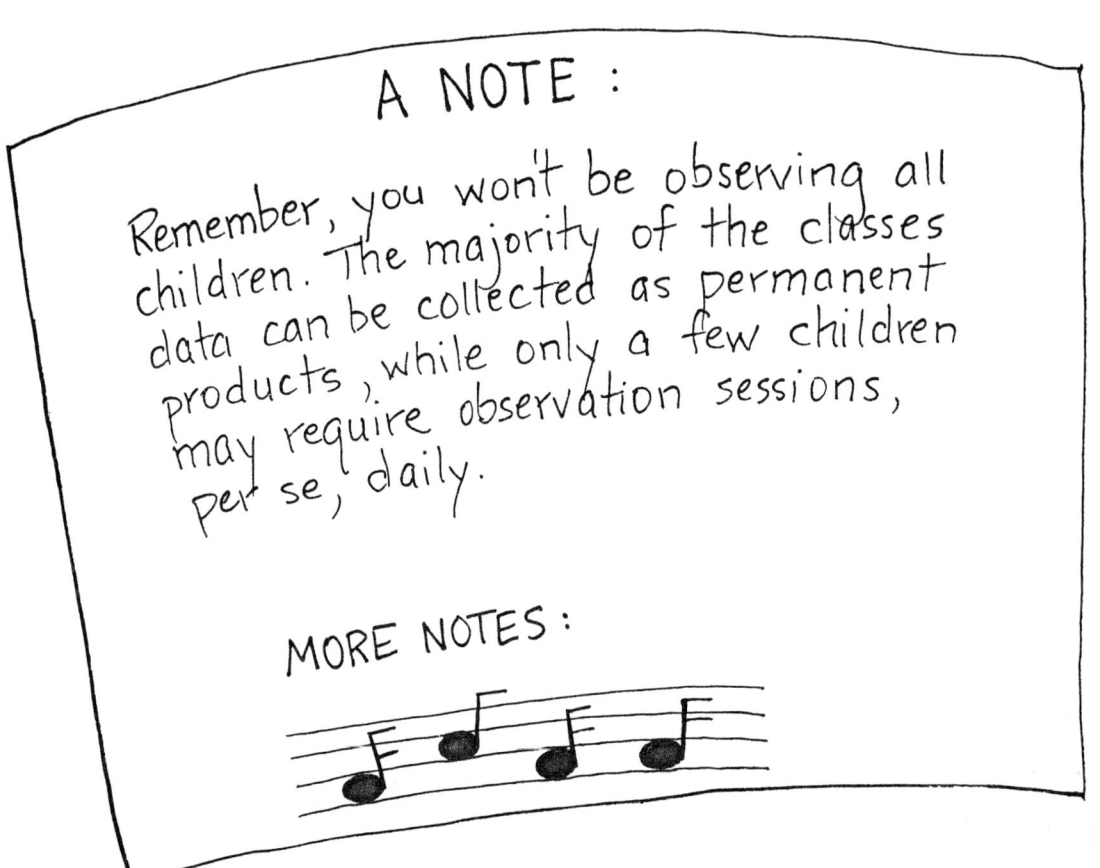

A NOTE:

Remember, you won't be observing all children. The majority of the classes data can be collected as permanent products, while only a few children may require observation sessions, per se, daily.

MORE NOTES:

Sometimes the measurement procedure is simply to count the number of times the behavior occurs. This procedure is good for behaviors which occur at a rate which is low enough not to cause any problems with accuracy. Some types of behaviors with which this procedure is acceptable are "out of seat behavior," the number of math problems a child can do in 10 minutes, the number of words a child can read in a list in 5 minutes, the number of times a child pushes another child, or the number of times a child reverses "b" and "d", etc.

One way to be sure of accuracy is to have another teacher or the classroom aide observe the same behavior. If you agree 90% of the time or better your observations are quite reliable (accurate). A way to calculate this "reliability" is to take the total number of agreements and divide by the total number of disagreements plus agreements. Then multiply this by 100 and you will get the percent of reliability.

If it is difficult to observe a particular behavior for any given time interval (like 15 minutes) another counting procedure may be used. This is helpful when no classroom aide is available and continuing teaching must occur simultaneously with our obsevations and measurement. The technique involved here is to observe the child only at the end of a given time period (e.g., every minute interval) and to record whether or not the child is engaged in the behavior at the end of each time segment. In this technique you do not record every occurrence of the behavior but rather whether it is or is not occurring when you are observing. During the interval when you are *not* observing, teaching may continue uninterrupted. In this situation a wrist/counter is helpful so that the occurrence of the behavior can be recorded with no classroom interruption.

Child's Name: _____ Date: _____
Time: _____ To _____
Behavior Observed: _____

20"	20"	20"	20"	20"	20"	20"	20"	20"

Gaze at clock and note at every 20" interval whether behavior is or is not occurring. (The columns could be changed to 60" if desired).

Some behaviors require other types of measurement. For example, you may want to record the percentage of correct math problems a child completes in a given time period. You simply figure out the percent correct and plot it on a graph. (Graphing will be described shortly.)

Some behaviors need a duration measure. In other words you are concerned with how long the behavior occurs rather than how often. These types of behavior may involve temper tantrums, attention span, on-task behavior, and others. For measuring this type of behavior you would need a stopwatch or a watch with a sweep-second hand. Note when the behavior starts and then time how long it occurs. Write this amount of time down and later plot it on a graph.

GRAPHS

Graphs are a practical way to summarize your data. They also give you a picture of the child's progress. At first graphing may seem confusing, but once you become used to it, the saying "A picture is worth a thousand words," will become clear.

There are a few simple rules to follow in preparing a graph.

1) Use graph paper. While this is not absolutely necessary, it does allow for easier plotting and increases accuracy when reading it.

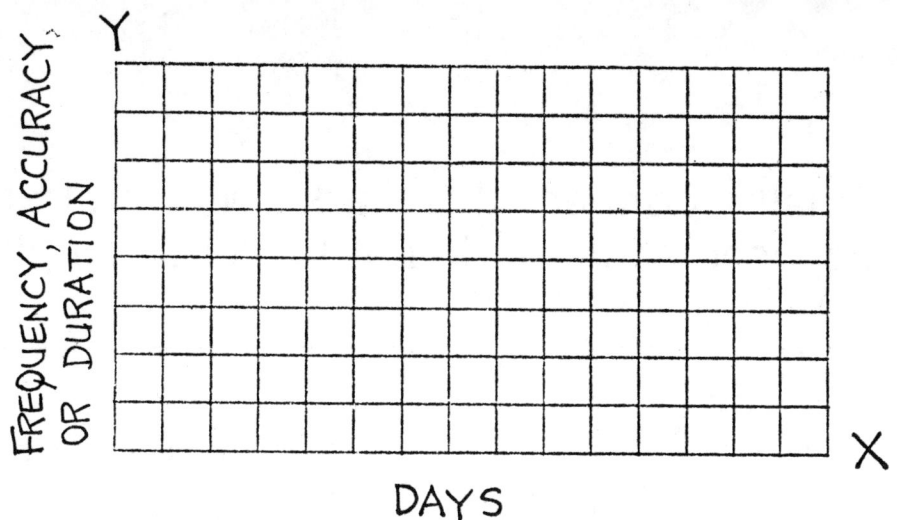

2) Always put the days on the X axis and the frequency, accuracy, or duration, on the Y axis.

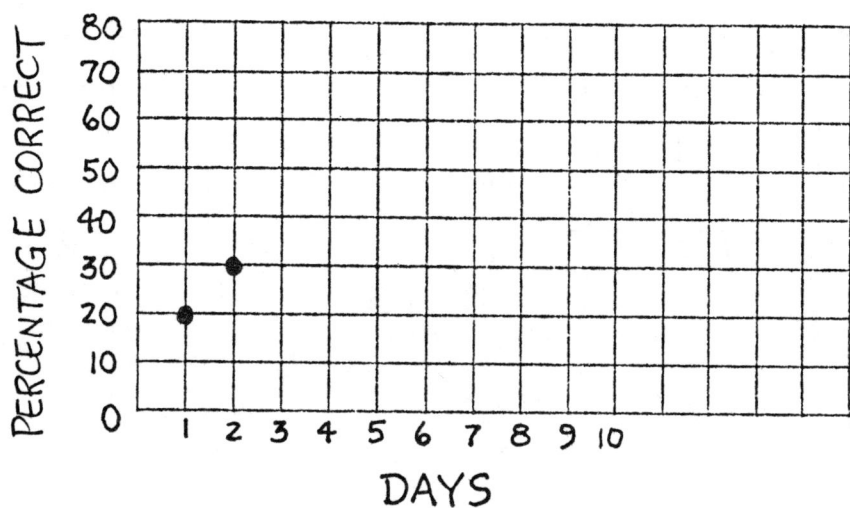

3) When marking the graph (plotting the data) start with your observations for day 1 and move up the Y axis to the appropriate number or percentage. For example, if on day 1 the child got 20% correct, mark above day 1 and up the Y axis 20%. For the next day mark above day 2 and up the Y axis to the correct percentage, say 30%.

4) Finally, connect the marks with a straight line between each mark. Let's read a sample graph.

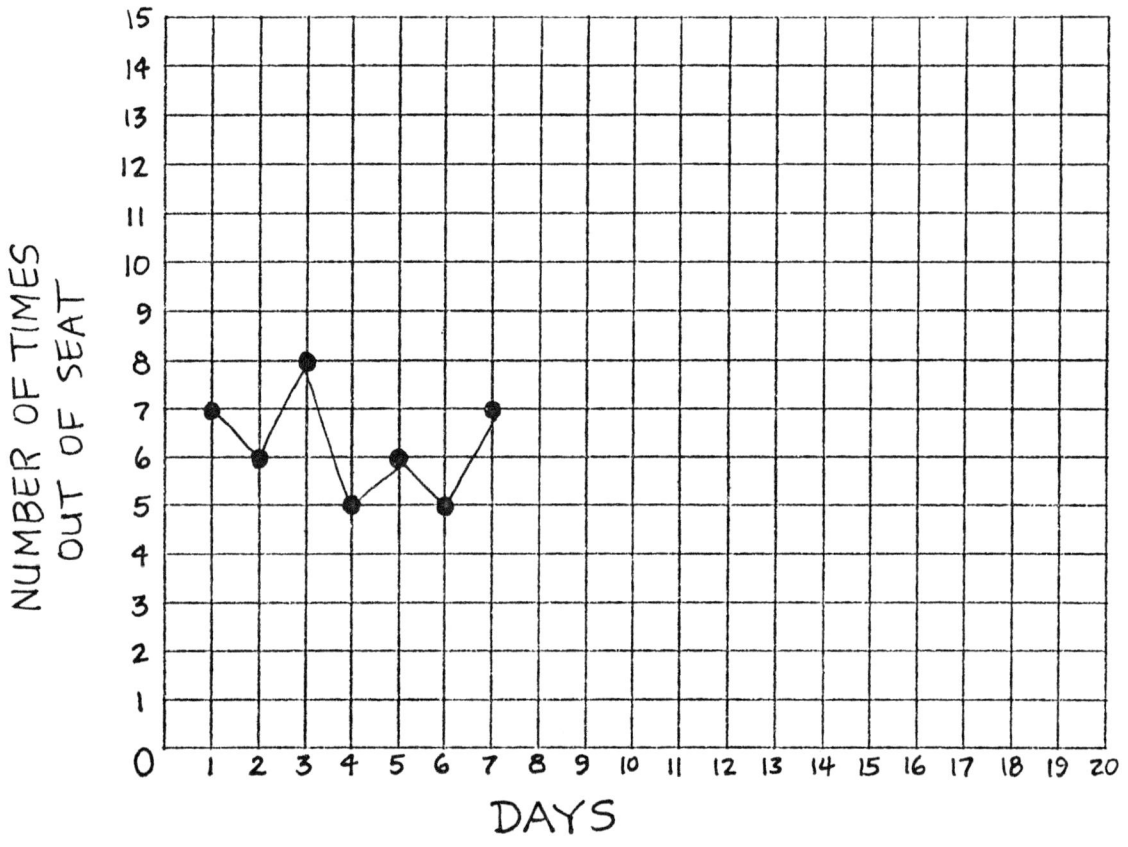

On day 1 you see the mark on 7, on day 2 it is 6, day 3 _____, day 4 _____, day 5 _____, day 6 _____, day 7 _____.
(Answers can be found on page 104).

Remember, the purpose of graphing the data is to evaluate your instructional or management strategy before it is too late and the child fails. However, before your evaluation can be valid, you must have a reference point. You can obtain this reference point (called baseline) by dividing your graph into sections. The first section will be around 5 days length. This may vary as what you look for is a steady rate across days. This is called stablity. On the average, 5 days shows stability, but only stop baseline and move on to your strategy when stability occurs. It could be more than 5 days! During these first several sessions you observe and record the data *before* you try your teaching strategy or change program. This baseline data is what you compare your observations with *after* you try your strategy. If you want to increase the accuracy of math responses, for example, and you see that relative to your baseline condition the accuracy does in fact increase then your strategy is working. If not, you must alter your strategy.

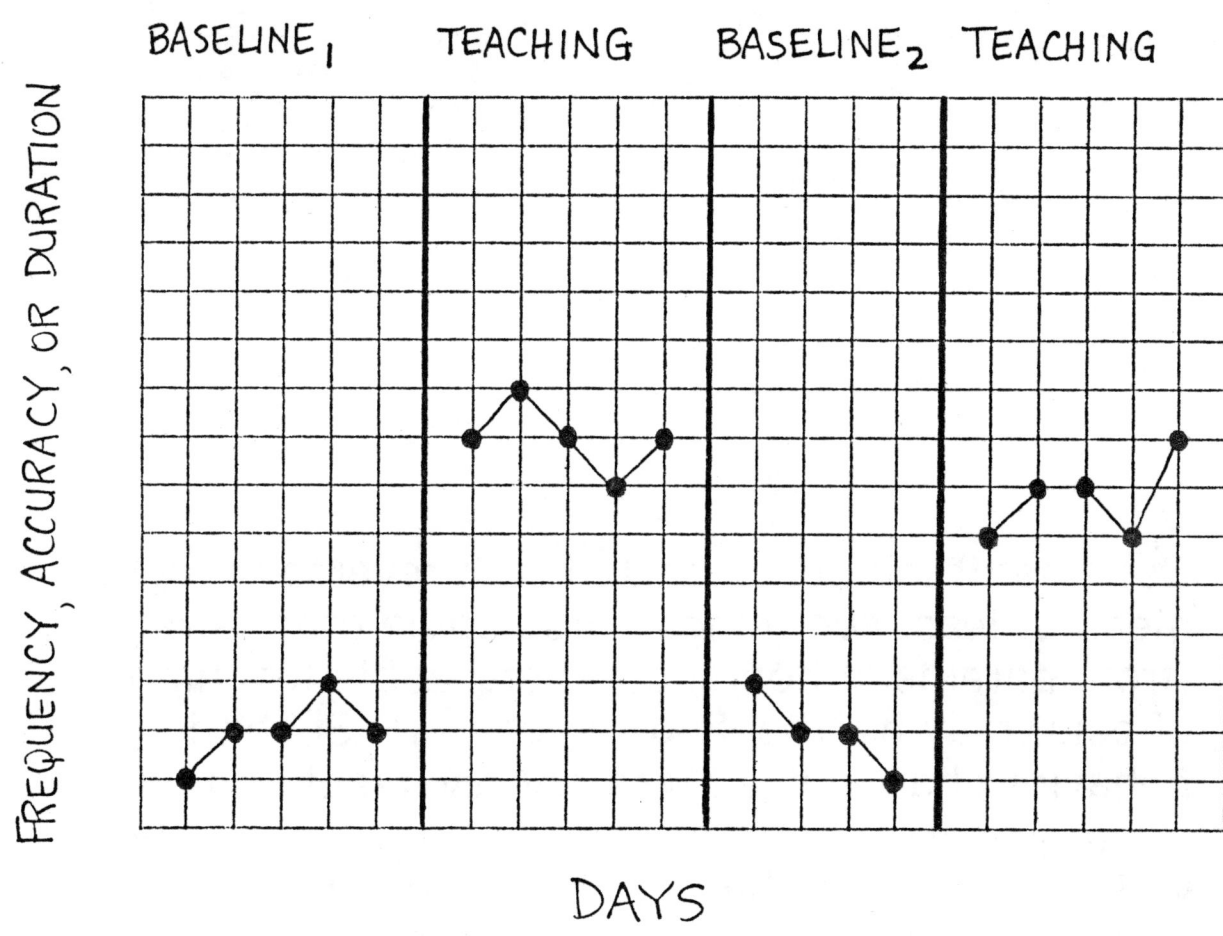

THE REVERSAL DESIGN

Depending upon how confident you want to be with attributing the change to your teaching strategies you may wish to remove the strategy and see if the behavior reverses back to conditions similar to baseline. If the behavior reverses back, you've found a good strategy. It works! This method is called a "reversal design."

But what if the behavior does not reverse? It could mean at least two things. First, some other strategy (from parents at home to generalizable teaching effects) may be affecting the change. Secondly, the behavior change itself was *not* reversable. Such behaviors are word recognition, (once a child learns a word it is doubtful he or she will unlearn it), maturationally induced behaviors, etc. The first possibility is beyond your control. The second, however, is handled by another design (other than the reversal design). This is called a multiple baseline design.

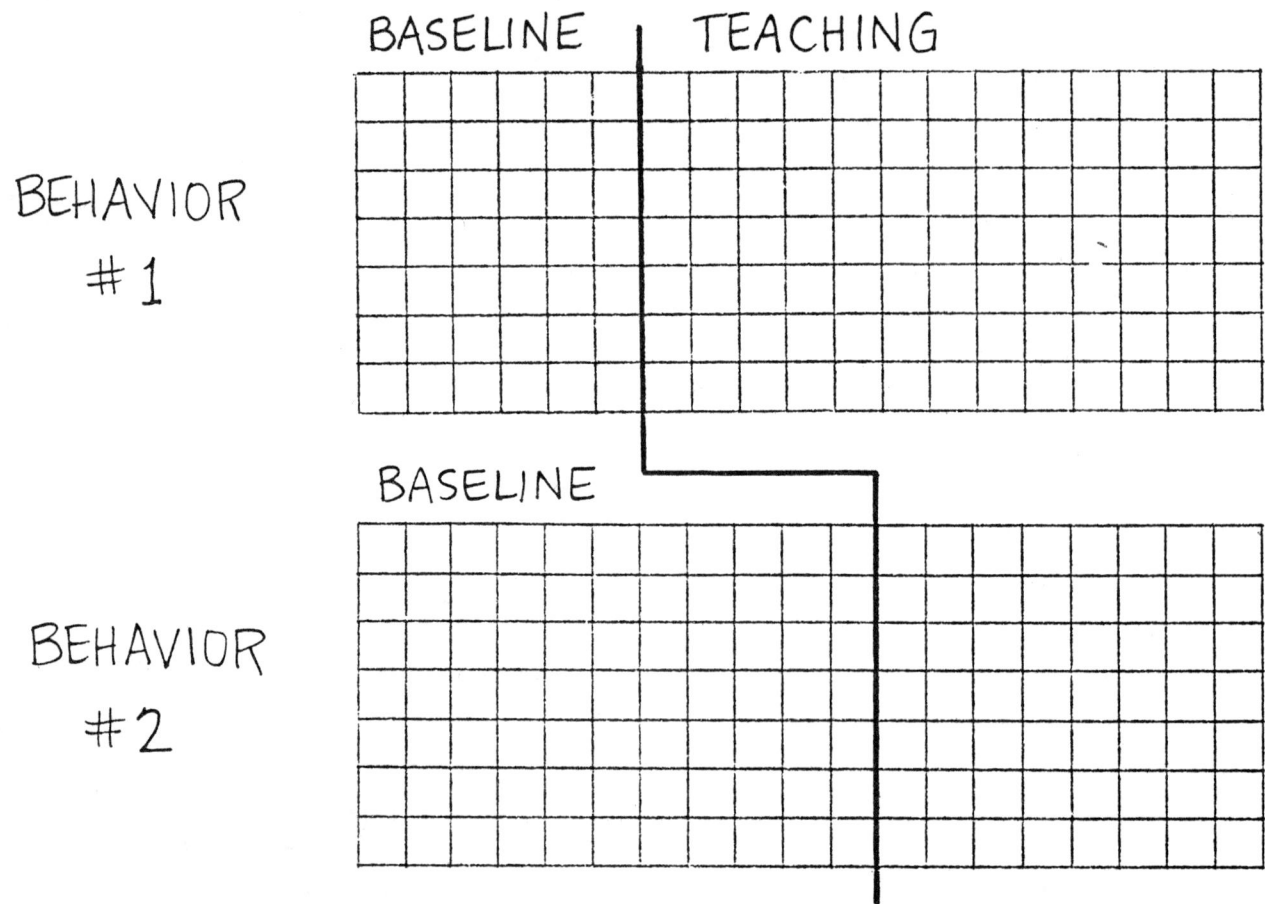

In the multiple baseline design you observe two behaviors in one child. After baseline collection you implement your strategy on one of the behaviors and not the other. If the behavior on which you try your strategy changes, but the other behavior stays steady during this period you adequately control the possibility of other strategies (parents, etc.) affecting the change. Again you have found a good strategy. (For an excellent source on measurement see Cooper, J. O., *Measurement and Analysis of Behavioral Techniques.* Columbus, Ohio: Merrill, 1974.)

An example of the use of a multiple baseline design might be in the area of sight word recognition. Since this behavior is probably irreversible (once the child learns the word it probably won't be unlearned) we will choose this design. We must pick another behavior which is similar to the sight recognition behavior for our "control." In this case we might choose number recognition as both skills require visual presentation and auditory recall.

Next we collect baseline on both behaviors. After stability occurs on the sight word recognition (approximately 5 days), we begin our teaching strategy on that behavior. The other behavior, number recognition, is kept on baseline (no strategy used). After we note an increase in sight word recognition (if our strategy is successful) and the baseline on number recognition remains relatively stable, then we can try the strategy on number recognition. If it increases then we have shown a strong functional relationship between our teaching strategy and the behaviors we worked with. Our strategy worked! (If our strategy does not work of course, we must try others until success is observed. If the second behavior increases while we're only working on the first behavior, don't worry about it too much, *but* you cannot be sure it was your strategy "causing" the effect!)

Teaching Strategies

If we want to increase behaviors we can use positive reinforcement along with shaping and prompting. If we want to decrease behaviors we can use negative reinforcement, and if necessary punishment. (Let's look at the area of increasing behaviors as we are usually dealing with academic behaviors. If you are dealing with social behavior problems please refer to *Behavior Disorders: Helping Children with Behavioral Problems,* by A. L. Parks, in the MAINSTREAMING SERIES.

Positive Reinforcement

Ideally you would want all children to be working at the level of "intrinsic" reinforcement. However, this is an unreal goal. You and I receive a lot of intrinsic reinforcement in the teaching profession, but let's face it, if your school district stopped your paychecks, you would probably try to find another position. The same is true of children.

Many children in your classroom are already working at that level of intrinsic reinforcement and probably need little more than an occasional "that's good work" to motivate them. Some children however, (and it turns out these children have learning problems) need more "concrete" reinforcers to motivate them.

Reinforcements can range from the intrinsic level all the way down to the primary (e.g., food) level. While some of the more severely involved children require food type reinforcers to motivate them (this is where the behavior modification and M & M's myth got started) most of the children in your class will be functioning at higher levels of reinforcement. The way to finding the appropriate level is to start with the higher levels and work down. This is important because if a child is *actually* functioning at a higher level and you put him/her on a lower one, then you will actually pull that child down and farther away from the intrinsic (ideal) level.

Typically one would start at the social level (praise, encouragement, approval) and work down to the secondary level. The secondary level consists of such things as stars, checkmarks, and tokens. When using these types of reinforcers, pair them with social reinforcers. This will help to move the child up to the social level. The teacher might say "Rhonda, that's really good work. You got 9 problems correct out of 10. That means you get another star." (The teacher had already informed the child that the stars could be traded in for an amount of "free time" in the science corner, for example.)

Only after many tries at these higher levels with little or no success should the primary level be used. Then after initial success, pair the primary reinforcers with social praise so that less primary reinforcers can be given. Tokens can be substituted for primary reinforcers and then be traded for primary reinforcers as part of the gradual changeover. Most times this changeover from primary reinforcers to other levels must be very gradual, otherwise learning will slow down or stop.

The way positive reinforcement is used in a teaching strategy is to present this reinforcement *immediately* after a correct response (behavior) occurs. Initially the reinforcers should be given after *every* correct response. After the correct responses begin to occur at a steady rate higher than baseline conditions, (after doing a reversal or multiple baseline design, discussed on pages 75-79) we must start lessening the number of times we present a reinforcing event. This will help the child move closer to the intrinsic level.

A help in this transition process is to pair the reinforcing events with social praise and on occasion present the social praise without the originally used reinforcers (stars, tokens, or whatever). Many times this goes smoothly. Sometimes, however it may not work.

For example the child might ask or demand "where's my token?" *Do not give the reinforcer if this occurs as you may possibly teach the child to demand tokens.* Instead say "maybe next time." If the child balks or makes a fuss over this response simply ignore it. *Possibly any attention given to the child in this situation will increase the likelihood of similar problems in the future.*

If this approach doesn't work, back down to a more continuous schedule of reinforcement (e.g., instead of giving 1 token for every 3 correct responses change it to 1 token for every 2 correct responses). Remember, just as with us, change is often gradual. Do not expect immediate results and only base your success on the data you've collected and graphed. Many times small changes you don't notice will show up when the behavior is recorded and graphed. This is the difference between feeling a change has occurred and observing ("knowing as a fact") a change has occurred.

So, what if you've tried all of this and you still are not having any success, where to next? Well, obviously a child cannot perform a correct response unless he/she knows how to.

Well, that's part of teaching. How do you get a child to see the word "bird" and say "bird" if you haven't taught him/her how? To get responses going you can use the techniques of "shaping," and "prompting."

Shaping

Shaping is reinforcing the child for responses that are close to the correct response. Initially the reinforced responses may not be very close to the desired criteria response, but as those responses become "better" you then require a little closer response before reinforcement is given. This is continued gradually until only closer and closer responses are reinforced. Then, finally, only the correct response is reinforced. As mentioned in *Mainstreaming the Gifted,* these approaches can be used in just the opposite manner to establish diverse (creative), rather than conforming behaviors. Some responses like 2 + 2 = 4 must be conforming, while others should be diverse like making up stories or using your imagination.

Prompting

Some children need to be "prompted" into getting a response going. For example, in order to get a child to print the letter "A" you might take the child's hand and put the child "through the motion" of printing the letter "A". After you take the child "through the motion," show him/her the product (printed "A") and praise or otherwise reinforce the child. After several times of putting the child "through the motion" you will notice the child doing some of the motion himself/herself. At this point release your motion a little and the more the child can do it alone, the more you release until finally you no longer are prompting the child. All children vary, some will require a more gradual transition than others.

The procedure just described can be viewed as a general teaching model applicable to most problem areas encountered by children with any learning problem. Let's take a look at some specific examples of how to apply the model in some of the more frequent problem areas.

Remember, your general model includes the following steps:

1. Setting specific objectives, including criteria level of "mastery."
2. Observing and measuring the behavior (including assessment)
3. Planning and implementing a teaching or change strategy
4. Evaluating the effectiveness of the strategy

With this in mind let's take a look at some academic problems in reading, writing, and math.

To begin with, reading is a very general area. We must break reading down into smaller tasks. Such tasks include readiness skills, phonics skills, structural skills, comprehension skills, and so on. Each of these areas can be broken down even further.

A sample objective for a child in the 1st grade would be to: say the short sound of the vowels A,E,I,O,U, when presented visually, with 98% accuracy.

Once you have determined your objective you must observe the behavior. This is sometimes called assessment. Probably one of the best methods of assessing specific academic tasks is through "teacher-made" tests. In this case you would simply take letter cards and place each vowel in front of the child and say, "what sound does this vowel make?" You simply record the child's responses and calculate the percent of accuracy. You also note which vowel the child vocalizes correctly and, if the child is correct 98% of the time on those vowels, you don't have to worry about teaching them. You do however, have to provide the opportunity for practice, because without practice the child may forget them.

Another point to remember is that this type of assessment is a form of baseline data collection and therefore the assessment must be repeated over several days until a steady rate occurs. The daily assessment may last only 5 minutes per day.

Next you must plan your teaching strategy. Be sure to include a reinforcing event immediately after a correct response occurs. One such strategy might be:

>Teacher presents letter and says, "This letter says "ĭ", can you say it?"
>
>Child: "ĭ"
>
>Teacher: "That's really good, try it again." (Gives child token)
>
>Teacher presents letter "i" again and says "What does this letter say?"
>
>Child: "ĭ"
>
>Teacher: "Good, you're learning fast" (Give child token).

You may limit each day's instruction to one letter so as not to confuse the child. At the end of each session re-assess the child's skills with the same technique you used during baseline. If improvement is noted continue until the child reaches the criterion level on all vowels.

Another problem area often encountered in the area of reading or writing is reversal problems. The "process" camp referred to in Chapter 3 attributes these reversals to perceptual problems or a lack of integration between the two cerebral hemispheres of the brain. Since this approach offers no solutions, it's more helpful to view the problem as poor form discrimination. Looking at it this way, you *can* plan an effective treatment strategy.

Your assumption is that the child does not know how to discriminate forms, so you will teach that skill.

Step 1 Objective: Given the letters R,S,d,b, the child will be able to copy them correctly, 98% of the time.

Step 2 Baseline: Present letter cards with each letter to the child and ask the child to write the letter. Repeat this until stability of performance occurs.

Step 3 Planning a Strategy Use a "matching to sample" procedure. The child is asked to circle the letter in the bottom row that is identical to top row.

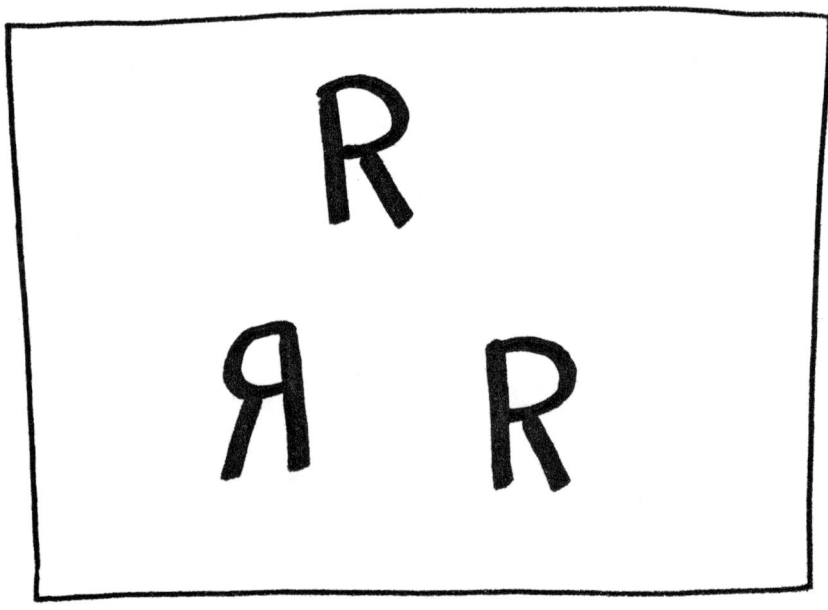

Be sure to reinforce correct responses with praise, and if necessary, tokens.

Step 4   Evaluate: After letting the child practice on the "matching to sample" procedure, conduct the same assessment you conducted during baseline. If the accuracy increases continue the procedure. If not...

Hold it! If not, you may have to prompt the behavior. Show the child the correct answer and say "see, the hump on the sample R points to the right. Which one in your answer points to the right?" If the child picks correctly reinforce his/her response. If not, you may have to back up and teach the child left from right!

Maybe you need to teach what a hand is.

Remember, each skill has a series of prerequisite skills that must be mastered before you can teach the skill in your objective.

So, part of your analysis must include breaking down the skills into their prerequisites and assessing if the child has those prerequisite skills in his/her behavioral repertoire. If not, they must be taught!

Let's look at an example of breaking a skill down:
    Given single digit addition problems the child will correctly answer them with 92% accuracy.

What prerequisite skills are necessary for the child to perform this objective?
A) The child must be able to correctly recognize the numbers 0-9.
B) The child must demonstrate that these numbers refer to a certain number of objects (this keeps the addition real rather than abstract).
C) The child must recognize that the symbol + means to combine.
D) If written problems, the child must be able to write the numbers.
E) Etc. Be thorough as there are other prerequisite skills that may be involved.

What we have attempted to do is to present an overview of a model with some examples as to how this problem-solving approach can be used. What was presented will hopefully get you started. If you wish to pursue this approach further a short annotated bibliography is included on the following page.

All children are unique, so they all cannot be taught in the same manner. While the average child may learn in spite of average teaching, an individualized approach must be used with kids having problems. The approach presented is a flexible model and will allow you to vary your methods of instruction to fit the uniqueness of the child. In doing so, we can make the classroom a pleasant place of learning for *all* children.

Day 3   8
Day 4   5
Day 5   6
Day 6   5
Day 7   7

Annotated Bibliography

Cooper, J.O. *Measurement and Analysis of Behavioral Techniques.* Columbus, Ohio: Merrill Publishing, 1974.

This book presents an excellent source for various observation techniques, methods of collecting data, methods of presenting and graphing data, and evaluation techniques to measure the effectiveness of teaching.

Engelmann, S. *Preventing Failure In the Primary Grades.* Chicago: SRA, 1969.

A practical book which gives explicit details as to how to help children with problems in reading and arithmetic.

Gardner, W. I. *Children with Learning and Behavior Problems, a Behavior Management Approach.* Boston: Allyn and Bacon, 1974.

A thorough but quite understandable presentation of the techniques of changing behavior. Procedures for implementing programs both at home and in the classroom are given. A list of audio-visual materials on these topics is also given.

Lowenbraun, S., and Affleck, J. Q. *Teaching Mildly Handicapped Children in Regular Classes.* Columbus, Ohio: Merrill Publishing, 1976.

After giving an overview of mainstreaming, the authors present very practical methods of teaching mildly handicapped children. Much emphasis is given on assessment techniques in the academic areas which is the strongest part of the book.

About the Authors

Thomas N. Fairchild, has his Ph.D. in School Psychology and is currently an Assistant Professor of Guidance and Counseling and Coordinator of the School Psychology Training Program at the University of Idaho. Dr. Fairchild earned his Bachelors, Masters, and Specialist degrees at the University of Idaho. He received his Ph.D. from the University of Iowa in 1974. The editor has published over a dozen journal articles in the areas of school psychology and counseling. Dr. Fairchild has worked as a teacher, counselor, and school psychologist. He has had the privilege of working with students across all grade levels, and in his opinion they are all special.

Dr. Ferris Henson received his Ph.D. in Special Education from the Ohio State University in 1974. While there, he studied in the areas of Mental Retardation, Learning Disabilities, and Clinical Psychology. He is presently teaching courses in the area of the gifted and is working on a federal grant dealing with mainstreaming.

Dr. Henson has one daughter, and aside from academic interests, is involved in music, handmade houses, gardening, and other "human" endeavors. His plans for the future include community involvement in the southern part of the U.S.A., and cross-cultural studies in special education in South America and Africa. However, he points out, "Plans for the future are quite fragile. Western science thought it had isolated most of life's variables only to find that there are many more we've never considered."

About the Illustrator

Everyone can draw—some with more competence than others. Occasionally you find someone who is exceptionally gifted in a particular facet of drawing. Danial B. Fairchild is that someone. He is a highly talented cartoonist with a style that is uniquely his own. His achievements include cartoons printed in newspapers and magazines, and most recently two paperbacks entitled **Cowtoons** (Artcraft Press, Nampa, Idaho), which depict, in a very humorous way, the life of cowboys.